CRITIQUE OF MARCUSE

Critique of Marcuse

by PAUL MATTICK

HERDER AND HERDER

New York   St. Louis   San Francisco

First American Edition
123456789BPBP79876543

Library of Congress Cataloging in Publication Data

Mattick, Paul, Date
Critique of Marcuse.
1. Marcuse, Herbert, 1898-   One dimensional man.
2. Civilization, Modern—20th century.   I. Title.
HM101.M269M3   1972   301.24′3   72-3941
ISBN 0-07-073785-1

I

"A Marxist shall not be duped by
any kind of mystification or illusion."
Herbert Marcuse

In an address delivered in Korcula, Yugoslavia,
Herbert Marcuse raised the question of "whether
it is possible to conceive of revolution when there is
no vital need for it." The need for revolution, he
explained, "is something quite different from a vital
need for better working conditions, a better income,
more liberty and so on, which can be satisfied within
the existing order. Why should the overthrow of the
existing order be of vital necessity for people who
own, or can hope to own, good clothes, a well-
stocked larder, a TV set, a car, a house and so on,
all within the existing order."[1] Marx, Marcuse
related, expected a working-class revolution because,
in his view, the labouring masses represented the

absolute negation of the bourgeois order. The accumulation of capital destined the workers to increasing social and material misery. They were thus both inclined and driven to oppose and to transform capitalist society. However, if the proletariat is no longer the negation of capitalism, then, according to Marcuse, "it is no longer qualitatively different from other classes and hence no longer capable of creating a qualitatively different society."[2]

Marcuse is fully aware of the social unrest in even the advanced capitalist nations and of actually or potentially revolutionary situations in many underdeveloped countries. However, the movements in advanced nations are movements for "bourgeois rights," as, for instance, the Negro struggles in the United States. And the movements in underdeveloped countries are clearly not proletarian but national whose purpose was overcoming foreign oppression and the backwardness of their own conditions. Although the contradictions of capitalism still persist, the Marxian concept of revolution no longer fits the actual situation, for, in Marcuse's view, the capitalist system has succeeded in "in channelling antagonisms in such a way that it can manipulate them. Materially as well as ideologically, the very classes which were once the absolute negation of the capitalist system are now more and more integrated into it."[3]

The meaning and extent of this "integration" Marcuse develops at length in his book *One Dimen-*

sional Man.[4] The integrated man lives in a society without opposition. Although bourgeoisie and proletariat are still its basic classes, the structure and function of these classes has been altered in such a way "that they no longer appear to be agents of historical transformation."[5] While the advanced industrial society is "capable of containing qualitative change for the foreseeable future," Marcuse does acknowledge that "forces and tendencies still exist which may break this containment and explode society."[6] In his view, "the first tendency is dominant, and whatever preconditions for a reversal may exist are being used to prevent it."[7] This situation may be altered accidentally, but "unless the recognition of what is being done and what is being prevented subverts the consciousness and the behaviour of man, not even a catastrophe will bring about the change."[8]

Not only is the working class written off here as an agent of historical change but so is its bourgeois opponent. It is as if a "class-less" society were emerging within class-society, for the former antagonists are now united in "an overriding interest in the preservation and improvement of the institutional *status quo.*"[9] And this is so, according to Marcuse, because technological development—transcending the capitalist mode of production—tends to create a totalitarian productive apparatus which determines not only the socially-needed occupations, skills, and attitudes, but also individual needs and aspirations.

It "obliterates the opposition between private and public existence, between individual and social needs," and it serves "to institute new, more effective, and more pleasant forms of social control and social cohesion."[10] In totalitarian technology, Marcuse says, "culture politics, and the economy merge into an omnipresent system which swallows up or repulses all alternatives. The productivity and growth potential of this system stabilize the society and contain technical progress within the framework of domination."[11]

Marcuse recognizes of course that there are large areas where these totalitarian tendencies of control and cohesion do not exist. But he regards this as merely a question of time, as these tendencies assert themselves "by spreading to less developed and even to pre-industrial areas of the world, and by creating similarities in the development of capitalism and communism."[12] Because technological rationality tends to become political rationality, Marcuse thinks that the traditional notion of the "neutrality of technology" must be given up, for any political change can "turn into qualitative social change only to the degree to which it would alter the direction of technical progress—that is, develop a new technology."[13]

It is clear that Marcuse is not realistically describing existing conditions but rather observable *tendencies* within these conditions. In his view, it is the unchallenged unfolding of the potentialities of the present system which *seems* to lead into the completely integrated totalitarian society. Preventing this development, Marcuse says, would now require that the oppressed classes "liberate themselves from themselves as well as from their masters."[14] To transcend established conditions presupposes transcendence *within* these conditions, a feat denied one-dimensional man in one-dimensional society. And thus Marcuse concludes that "the critical theory of society possesses no concepts which could bridge the gap between the present and the future; holding no promise and showing no success, it remains negative."[15] In other words, the critical theory—or Marxism—is now merely a *beau geste*.

II

By refusing to accept the apparently unchangeable conditions of a new "barbarism," which arrogantly regards itself as the very height of civilization, Marcuse turns his negativism into effective social criticism, which remains valid even though the general tendencies derived from it may not come to pass, or may not come to pass in the way foreseen by him. Although one may not share his excessive "pessimism" as regards the "foreseeable future," this pessimism is nonetheless warranted in view of existing conditions.

Usually, in the past as well as today, hope for a socialist working-class revolution is given up in the expectation that social problems are solvable by way of reforms within the confines of capitalism. In this view, revolution has become not only highly improbable but entirely unnecessary. The rise of one-dimensional society and one-dimensional man is not only not bewailed but is celebrated as the common achievement of labour and capital to the benefit of all of society. Marcuse differentiates himself from such "critics" of Marxism and the proletarian revolution by opposing the "final" results of the reformist endeavours. For him, the world is in a bad and hopeless state just because there was not, and apparently will not be, a proletarian revolution, just because Marxism proved no match for the resilience of capitalism and for its capacity not only to absorb the revolutionary potentialities of the working class but to turn them to its own advantage.

In view of the present situation in the advanced capitalist nations, history seems to validate "Marxian" revisionism rather than revolutionary Marxism. The latter was the product of a period of development in which capital accumulation was indeed a period of increasing misery for the labouring population.

Around the turn of the century, however, it became clear that in its decisive aspects the Marxian prognosis deviated from the real development; i.e., capitalism did not imply the continuous impoverishment of the working-class, and the workers themselves, far from becoming more class-conscious, were increasingly more satisfied with the steady improvement of their conditions within the capitalist system.

The war of 1914 revealed that the working class had ceased being a revolutionary force.

The miseries of war and of the prolonged depression in its wake revived to some extent the oppositional inclinations of the working class, and the spectre of social revolution stalked the world again. But capitalism once more proved able to side-track the released revolutionary energies and to utilize them in pursuit of its own ends. Practically and ideologically, the Second World War and its aftermath led to an almost total eclipse of working-class socialism. There is no point in denying this obvious fact. It is true, nonetheless, that the absence of any effective opposition to the capitalist system presupposes the system's ability to steadily improve the living conditions of the labouring population. If it should turn out that this is not a continuous process, the present "cohesion" of the capitalist system may well be lost again—as it has been lost in previous crises of long duration.

Marcuse bases his pessimism on what appears to him to be capitalism's newly-gained ability to solve economic problems by political means. In his view, *laissez-faire* capitalism with its crisis-cycle has been successfully transformed into a "regulated profit economy, controlled by the state and the large monopolies, into a system of organized capitalism."[16] He assumes that this system is able constantly to increase production and productivity, particularly through the instrumentalities of automation, and will thus be able to continue to maintain high living standards for its workers. There exists, Marcuse thinks, actual and potential "abundance," which, though accompanied by an unprecedented "degree of concentration of cultural, political, and economic power," satisfies men's material needs sufficiently so as to extinguish their desire for social change and to evoke a "world of identification."

The possibility of an "organized capitalism" either pleased or worried many social theoreticians. For instance, this idea supported Rudolf Hilferding's theory of the formation of a *General Cartel*,[17] in which production was completely organized while based on an antagonistic system of distribution. Such a non-competitive capitalism, though perhaps conceivable on a national scale, is entirely inconceivable as a world-wide system and, for that reason, would be only partially realizable on the national level. What national capitalist organization arose was mainly in response to international competition, and the more that "planning" entered into, and transformed, the market mechanism, the more chaotic and destructive the capitalist system became. Capitalistic property relations preclude any effective form of social organization of production, and it is only where these property relations have been destroyed, as in Russia for instance, that it proved possible, in some measure, to organize social production centrally on the basis of an antagonistic system of distribution. But even here, the character of the planned economy is still co-determined by international competition and to that extent represents an "organization" which helps perpetuate the general anarchy of capital production.

Marcuse describes this situation as the co-existence of communism and capitalism, "which explains both the metamorphosis of capitalism and the disfigurement which the original idea of socialism has undergone in practice."[18] While this co-existence precludes the full realization of socialism, he also sees it as the "driving power" behind the general growth of productivity and production. It impels capitalism, he says, " to stabilize itself and hence it brings social integration within capitalist society; there is a suspension of antitheses and contradictions within the society."[19] Now, there can be no doubt that in both the so-called communist nations and in capitalism proper productivity has been increased and will be further increased with continued technological development. But this does not necessarily lead to greater stabilization and social integration; it can have, and in our view, must have, quite opposite results.

III

Aside from the fact that even without co-existence competitive capital accumulation generates enough "driving power" to increase the productivity of labour, it should be clear that the dynamics of capital production are not identical with technological development. It is not production and productivity as such which propel capitalism, but the production of profits as the accumulation of capital. For instance, it is not a physical inability to produce which leads to a decline of production in a crisis situation, but the inability to produce profitably. The commodity glut on the market indicates the difference between production and capitalist production. It is, then, not the technical power to produce "abundance" which determines the state of the capitalist economy, but merely the power—or the lack of it—to produce an abundance of profit. A technology of actual or potential "abundance" does not imply a real abundance capable of satisfying existing social needs.

To be sure, the real wages of workers have increased in modern times. But only under conditions of capital expansion, which implies that the relationship between wages and profit remains generally the same. The productivity of labour rose fast enough to allow for both capital accumulation and a higher standard of living. In periods of depression there was a temporary reversal of this trend. Where capital did not accumulate, living standards either declined, or remained what they were prior to the emergence of capitalism. According to Marx—whose theory of capitalist development it is assumed the reader is acquainted with—capital accumulation leads necessarily to a decline of profitability relative to the growing mass of capital, and therewith to crises and depressions devastating enough to produce social convulsions and, eventually, the overthrow of the capitalist system. But Marx's "general law of capitalist accumulation," derived as it is from highly abstract considerations of capitalism's structure and dynamics, was not provided with a time-table. The contradictions of capital production could come to a head sooner or later—even much later.

Difficulties in the production of capital are, of course, concretely countered by all available means capable of restoring a required profitability, which, if successful, assure the continued existence of capitalism. But a mere increase in production is not a sign of capitalist expansion; it is such only when issuing into capital formation, and by doing so in accelerating measure. Although there is an enormous increase in production in times of war, it is accompanied by an excessively low rate of capital formation. Surplus-labour, instead of being capitalized in additional profit-yielding means of production, is utilized in the production of waste and for the destruction of capital already accumulated. Likewise, in times of "peace," production may be increased despite a stagnating or declining rate of capital formation by way of compensatory government-induced production. The prevalence of the "mixed economy" is an admission that capitalism would find itself in a depression if it were not for the expanding government-determined sector of the economy.

As far as *laissez-faire* capitalism is concerned, Marx's prediction of its decline and eventual demise is obviously still supported by the actual capitalist development. Marcuse, too, insists, that "the economy can only function because of the direct or indirect intervention of the State in vital sectors."[20] But what does this intervention imply as regards the private-enterprise economy? No doubt, it increases production and, by means of this increase, expands the productive apparatus beyond what it would be without State intervention. In so far as there is capital accumulation it is made possible through government. The latter avails itself of productive resources not its own by purchasing certain products from private enterprise. If the goal of these transactions is the stabilization of the market economy, government-induced production must be non-competitive. If the government would purchase consumption goods and durables in order to give them away, it would, to the extent of its purchases, reduce the private market demand for these commodities. If it would produce either of these commodities in government-owned enterprises and offer them for sale, it would increase the difficulties of its private competitors by reducing their shares of a limited market demand. Government purchases, and the production it entails, must fall out of the market system; it must be supplementary to market production. It is therefore predominantly concerned with goods and services that have no place in the market economy, that is, with public works and public expenditures of all descriptions.

The division between private and public production is, of course, not absolute. Political exigencies induce governments to enter the sphere of private market production, for instance, by subsidizing certain commodities and by purchasing surplus products to be utilized in foreign and domestic aid projects. There is some over-lapping of private and public business activities in various branches of production as well as in their marketing and financing. Generally, however, one can speak of the division of the economy into a profit-determined private sector, and a smaller, non-profitable, public sector. The private sector must realize its profits through market transactions, the public sector operates independently of the market, even though its existence and its activities affect the private sector's market relations.

The government increases the "effective demand" through purchases from private industry, either financed with tax money or by borrowings on the capital market. In so far as it finances its expenditures with tax money, it merely transfers money made in the private sector to the public sector, which may change the character of production to some extent but does not necessarily enlarge it. If the government borrows money at the capital market, it can increase production through its purchases. But this increase in production increases the national debt by way of deficit-financing.

Capital exists either in "liquid" form, i.e., as money, or in fixed form, that is, as means and materials of production. The money borrowed by government puts productive resources to work. These resources are private property, which, in order to function as *capital,* must be reproduced and enlarged. Depreciation charges and profits gained in the course of government-contracted production—not being realizable on the market—are "realized" out of the money borrowed by the government. But this money, too, is private property—on loan to the government at a certain rate of interest. Production is thus increased, the expense of which piles up as government indebtedness.

To pay off its debts and the interest on them, the government has to use tax money, or make new borrowings. The expense of additional, government-contracted production is thus carried by private capital, even though it is distributed over the whole of society and over a long period of time. In other words, the products which the government "purchases" are not really purchased, but given to the government free, for the government has nothing to give in return but its credit standing, which, in turn, has no other base than the government's taxing-power and its ability to increase the supply of credit-money. We will not enter here into the intricacies of this rather complex process, for however the credit expansion is brought about, and however it is dealt with in the course of an expanding government-induced production, one thing is clear, namely, that the national debt, and the interest on it, cannot be honoured save as a reduction of current and future income generated in the private sector of the economy.

If not caused by war, government intervention in the economy finds its reason in the malfunction of private capital production. The latter is not profitable enough to assure its self-expansion, which is a precondition for the full use of its productive resources.

Profitability cannot be increased by way of non-profitable production; in so far as capital produces without regard to profitability it does not function as capital. Although its unused productive capacities are put to use by government contracts, "profits" made in this way, and "capital accumulated" in this process are mere book-keeping data relating to the national debt, and not actual profit-yielding new means of production, even where the physical productive apparatus grows with the increase in production. A relatively faster increase in government-induced production than total social production implies the relative decline of private capital formation. The decline is covered-up by the increase in production to government account, the "profits" of which take on the form of claims on the government.

Because government-induced production is itself a sign of a declining rate of capital formation in the traditional sense, it cannot be expected to serve as the vehicle for an expansion of private capital effective enough to assure conditions of full employment and general prosperity. It rather turns into an obstacle to such expansion, as the demands of government on the economy, and the old and new claims on the government, divert an increasing part of the newly-produced profit from its capitalization to private account.

Of course, claims on the government, which make up the national debt, can be repudiated, and "profits" made via government-induced production are thus revealed for what they actually are, namely, imaginary profits. But though perhaps unavoidable some day, governments, representing private capital, will postpone this day as long as possible, particularly, because the repudiation of debts alone does not guarantee the resumption of a profitable private capital accumulation. Meanwhile, of course, there is a slow but steady depreciation of incomes and debts by way of inflation—a necessary process connected with the expansion of government-induced production by way of deficit-financing.

Notwithstanding the long duration of rather "prosperous" conditions in the industrially-advanced countries, there is no ground for the assumption that capital production has overcome its inherent contradictions through State interventions in the economy. The interventions themselves point to the persistency of the crisis of capital production, and the growth of government-determined production is a sure sign of the continuing decay of the private-enterprise economy. To arrest this decay would mean to halt the vast expansion of government-induced production and to restore the self-expansive powers of capital production; in short, it implies a reversal of the general developmental trend of twentieth-century capitalism. As this is highly improbable, the State will be forced to extend its economic inroads into the private sectors of the economy and thus become itself the vehicle for the destruction of the market economy. But where the State represents private capital, it will do so only with great hesitation and against growing opposition on the part of private capital. This hesitation may be enough to change the conditions of an apparent "prosperity" into conditions of economic crisis.

Marcuse does recognize that there are "conflicts between the private and state sectors" of the economy, but he does not think "that this is one of the explosive conflicts which could lead to the destruction of capitalism"; particularly not, he says, because these conflicts "are nothing new in the history of capitalism."[21] There was always opposition, of course, to government controls as exemplified in *laissez-faire* ideology, yet the present objective conflict between government and business is of a different character because of the relatively faster growth of the government-determined production in the course of the general expansion of capital. The quantitative change points to an undesired, yet inescapable, qualitative change. Private capital must oppose this change with the same determination with which it opposes socialism itself, for an extensive State control of the economy forecasts the end of private enterprise. It is for this reason that capitalism opposes state-capitalist systems as if they were socialist regimes, for, from their interest-position, one equates with the other, no matter how far removed the nationally-organized state-capitalist (or state-socialist) system actually is from the "original concept of socialism."

The objective opposition between state-control and private capital production is still clouded and appears as the subjective cooperation of business and government in the nominally market-determined economy. This "cooperation," however, is possible only because it still subordinates government policies to the specific needs of big business. But the specific needs of big business contradict the general needs of society, and the social conflicts thereby released will turn into conflicts about the role of government in economic affairs, that is, will be political struggles for the control of government in order either to restrict, or to extend, its interventions in the economy. This struggle *transcends*—either backward or forwards—the established conditions and does so *within* these conditions.

IV

Capitalism will not turn itself into socialism. But neither can it maintain itself indefinitely as a "mixed economy," wherein government solves the problems of capital production by political means. Government intervention in the capitalist economy is itself restricted by the limitations of capital production. The organization of social production presupposes the expropriation of private capital. It will be just as difficult, however, to make a state-capitalist revolution as it is to make a socialist revolution. But short of the nationalization of productive resources, all state interventions in the market economy—while perhaps raising production to the extent of these interventions—will increase the difficulties of competitive capital formation in the foreseeable future.

According to Marx, definite social relations—or production relations—correspond to definite social productive forces released by them and bound to their existence. The capital-labour relationship determines the unfolding of technological development as the accumulation of capital. Only within the frame of capital formation do science and technology expand the capacities of social production by increasing the productivity of labour. Under the social relations of capital production the given potentialities of socialized production cannot be fully realized, since their realization would destroy existing capitalist production relations. At a certain point in its development, capital becomes a hindrance to a further unfolding of the social forces of production, and, from the point of view of production, changes from a progressive into a regressive force. Only destruction of the capitalist system can now assure continued progressive social development.

Marcuse himself points out that in Marxian theory "the social mode of production, not technics, is the basic historical factor."[22] He deviates from this position however, although reluctantly, by noting that society "sustains its hierarchic structure while exploiting ever more efficiently the natural and mental resources, and distributing the benefits of this exploitation on an ever-larger scale."[23] In other words, Marcuse thinks that capitalism can continue to develop the social forces of production and still maintain its class structure. In his view, it is not capitalism's class character which hinders technical development, it is technology rather which secures the continued existence of capitalism.

"Technical progress, technology itself," Marcuse says, "have become a new system of exploitation and domination,"[24] a system which is no longer challenged but willingly, or passively, accepted by all social classes. But at this point, Marcuse remains ill at ease, for he also says "that technology is not the major factor responsible for this situation."[25] Technic and technological development, he explains, "is a system of domination . . . organized in such a way that the existing (social) system in the highly industrial capitalist countries is very largely held together by them."[26]

For Marcuse, the present technology is specific to,

but not limited by, capitalism. It offers a way
out for capitalism and is therefore the most important obstacle to its abolition. For Marx, too,
science and technology are specific to capitalism,
but only in the sense that their direction and development find their determination and limitations in
capitalist relations of production. Should these
relations be abolished, science and technology could
take on an unhampered and different course, in
accordance with the conscious and rational decisions
of fully-socialized man. For Marx, it is neither
science nor technology which constitutes a system of
domination, but it is the domination of labour by
capital which—with everything else—turns science
and technology into instrumentalities of exploitation
and class rule. In Marcuse's view, however, it is no
longer capitalism which determines the state and
nature of technology; it is technology which determines the state and nature of capitalism.

Marcuse thinks that "Marx did not foresee tech-
nologically advanced society . . . nor all the things
which capitalism could accomplish . . . simply by
exploiting its technical breakthroughs."[27] Yet, all that
capitalism can accomplish in this way, even in
Marcuse's view, is its own maintenance by keeping
technological progress within the boundaries of class
domination. But as this technology finds—by and
large—the support of all layers of society by satisfying their material needs, it can assure its domina-

tion over, and its growth within, class society.

Marcuse's statement that "Marx did not foresee technologically-advanced society" is hardly justifiable in view of Marx's projection of social development toward the "abolition of labour" through the unfolding of the social forces of production, which include science and technology. But it is true that Marx did not believe that much in this direction could be done within the confines of capitalism, which was an additional reason for calling for its abolition.

The utopian "abolition of labour" implies the abolition of capitalism, or of any other successive form of class exploitation. This actually unreachable goal only serves to indicate the general direction which social development must take in order to decrease necessary labour-time in favour of freetime. The "abolition of labour" is not only an unreachable but also an inhuman goal, for it was labour itself which differentiated man from animal and created humanity. The "abolition of labour" has meaning only as the progressive abolition of necessary, or forced, labour. Free-time can also be "labourtime," freely engaged in, in the pursuit of a variety of individual and social ends. But free-time in this sense presupposes a reduction in the labour-time necessary to sustain social life, and requires an increasing productivity of labour through the labours of science and technology.

Socialism was, then, conceived as the end of exploitation and the freeing of the social forces of production from their capitalist fetters, so as to assure a maximum of free-time. Socialism itself presupposed the socialist revolution. Marcuse thinks it timely, however, to question the continuing validity of the (Marxian) concept that "the realm of work remains the realm of necessity, whereas the realm of liberty can only develop above and beyond the realm of necessity," because, in his view, "the end of necessary work is in sight; it is not a utopia; it is a real possibility."[28]

To be sure, Marcuse is careful to make his prognostications in the form of questions. He asks, for instance, "What does it mean when, in mass technological society—work-time—socially-necessary time—is reduced to a minimum and free time practically becomes full time?"[29] Although he only raises the question, the question itself seems to imply the possibility of the emergence of such a state of affairs. But placed in context with capitalism, these are false questions. The technical revolution required to eliminate work-time in favour of free-time is not compatible with capitalism.

Capital is congealed surplus-labour in the form of surplus-value, and it feeds and expands on living labour. In so far as technological development is a function of capital formation in value terms, the capital accumulated in the materialization of unpaid labour-time. The reduction of labour-time, not to speak of its abolition, also implies the reduction of unpaid labour-time, and therewith the reduction of capital formation. To be sure, unpaid labour-time can be increased at the expense of paid labour-time, even while total labour-time is decreased, through the increase of labour productivity in the course of capital expansion. As less labour-time is needed to produce the commodity-equivalent of the workers' income, more of the total labour-time can take on the form of products appropriated by the capitalists. But the continuous reduction of labour-time must eventually also reduce unpaid labour-time and thus stop the process of capital expansion by way of the increasing productivity of labour. Where there is no labour, there can be no surplus-labour and, consequently, no accumulation of capital.

Whatever the extent of automatization and computerization, means of production neither operate nor reproduce themselves. On the quite improbable assumption that their owners, the capitalists, engaged themselves in production, they would thereby cease being capitalists, that is, buyers of labour-power for purposes of exploitation. Assuming, what is more probable, that they succeed in continuously reducing the number of productive workers, they would also reduce the unpaid labour-time relative to the mass of the accumulated capital. It will then become increasingly more difficult to continue the capital formation process, which is only the accumulation of unpaid labour-time transformed into profit-yielding new means of production.

Capital-labour relations are value relations, which is to say, that means of production are not that only but are also capital values, and that labour-power is not that only but is also the source of value and surplus-value. To consummate the capitalist production process, surplus-value must have a definite relation to the value of capital, i.e., it must be sufficient to ensure its enlarged reproduction. As value-relations are labour-time relations, it should be clear—at least to the Marxist—that a reduction in labour-time which would disturb the necessary relationship between surplus-value and capital is not compatible with capitalism and will, for that reason, interrupt, or end, the capitalist production process.

V

To argue in this manner is to argue, however, on a very high level of abstraction. It is in this way that the basic social relationships behind the capitalistic economic categories can be brought to light. But these relationships, while determining the boundaries of capital production, do not affect capitalistic behaviour. And thus, while the reduction of social labour-time becomes a detriment to capital production, the reduction of labour-costs remains a necessary requirement for each single enterprise, or corporation. Their profitability increases as their labour-costs diminish. It is for this reason that the displacement of labour by capital cannot be halted within the competitive capital formation process, even though it undermines the very structure of capitalist society.

All social progress is based on the ability to produce more with less labour. Capitalism is no exception. Technological development always displaces labour, which is only another way of saying that production increases through an increase in productivity. A rapid rate of capital formation, however, can increase the absolute number of workers while decreasing this number relative to the growing capital. It is only under conditions of relative capital stagnation that advancing technology diminishes the number of workers absolutely.

Increasing productivity manifests itself not only in a diminishing number of workers relative to the growing mass of capital, but also in the reduction of their working-time. More can be produced in a shorter than in a longer work-period, through changes in work-techniques and machine technology. The reduction of working-time is only another expression for the increase in real wages, and has been thrust upon the capitalists by way of labour struggles as well as by the rationality of modern methods of production.

While capitalism feeds on labour and transforms the bulk of the population into wage workers, it also constantly decreases the number of labourers and their labour-time relative to the mass of commodities they are able to produce. While, on the one hand, capitalism aspires to the maximum of surplus-value, or surplus-labour, on the other hand, a minimum of labour must produce a maximum of commodities. The "ideal" would be, of course, to get the maximum of surplus-labour from the greatest number of workers, but this "ideal" conflicts with the realities of capital production and the circulation process to which it gave rise.

The separate capital entities produce for the market and realize their profits through the sale of their commodities. There is competition and thus a constant pressure to reduce production costs, which, for each capitalist enterprise, means mainly labour costs. The pressure is relieved through technological innovations, which allow the same, or a smaller, amount of labour to produce more commodities than before. The process is reflected in a change of the relationship between capital and labour, since relatively fewer workers attend to a greater amount of capital in the form of means of production.

In abstract value terms, a more rapid rise of the capital invested in means of production than that invested in labour-power depresses the rate of profit, which is measured on total capital. But this need not, and does not, worry the capitalists, who will realize their customary profits on their capital if they succeed in selling their increased production at competitive prices. The greater production of the labour employed more than compensates for the relative decline of labour through technological development, and the accumulation process can proceed.

There is no reason to assume, however, that an increase in production automatically enlarges the market, nor that the *tendency* of falling profitability in the course of capital formation is automatically overcome through the increasing productivity of labour. Things may not fall together to assure a frictionless capital expansion. The increasing productivity of labour may not be sufficient to counteract the downward pressure of the rate of profit through the structural changes of capital; profits made in production may not be realizable on the market; and a whole host of other difficulties may retard, or interrupt, the capital formation process. In any case, until recently the development of capitalism has been punctuated by periods of depression of increasing severity and duration.

To the capitalists, economic difficulties appear as marketing problems, as a lack of effective demand, which leads to reduced production and unemployment. There is no incentive for further capital expansion. The ensuing stagnation, or depression, while destroying many businesses improves the profitability of the survivors by presenting them with larger markets. A more concentrated capital now commands a larger sphere of business operations. It defends and consolidates the newly-won position through the cutting of labour-costs, by investing anew in technological innovations. To a greater or lesser degree, competition forces all capitals to do the same and a new wave of investments, altering the relationship between profit and wages, initiates a new period of capital production. The problems of capitalism, coming to the fore on the market, find their solutions in the sphere of production, even though the solution is not complete until it also affects market relations.

This brief description does not do justice to the complexity of the business-cycle. But it must suffice here to indicate that basically it is a problem of profit production. Each new upswing after a period of depression increases production far beyond what it was before. The conditions of production prior to the depression removed the incentives for capital expansion, and the lack of such expansion depressed the economy sufficiently to cause a glut on the market, a lack of buying-power, or a lack of effective demand. The much larger production in the upswing period finds its buying-power in the capital expansion process itself, as it once more becomes viable through a change in the conditions of production, which raise the profitability of capital.

What are considered conditions of prosperity are conditions of continuous capital expansion. Without them depression prevails. In the past, depression was a pre-condition of prosperity and the latter led invariably into a new depression. It was in this manner that capital "reorganized" itself by way of market events—bringing forth changes in the conditions of production—without conscious interferences in its market mechanism. But changes in the conditions of production—capital-labour relations, that is—make similar future changes increasingly more difficult as capital increases in mass which in turn requires an always accelerating increase in productivity in order to overcome its inherent tendency of decreasing profit-rates through the structural changes brought forth by capital accumulation.

However, *laissez-faire* capitalism has been succeeded by what Marcuse calls "organized capitalism," and it could well be that the dynamics of the "old" capitalism, issuing into increasingly more devastating depressions, have lost their validity for the "new" capitalism, characterized by monopolistic features and extensive government interventions in the economy.

With government interventions we have dealt before. As regards monopoly, it "organizes" nothing but the particularistic interests of monopoly capital within competitive capitalism, and while avoidable, is nonetheless a disintegrating, not an integrating, factor of capitalist development.

Monopoly is always accompanied by competition. It is itself only a form of competition. Monopoly, i.e., the prevalence of monopolistic, administered prices, relates to the total market situation. The higher the monopoly price, the smaller will be the demand for commodities offered at that price, for the market demand is itself limited by the total social income. Moreover, what is being "over-paid" in the monopoly price cannot be spent on commodities subjected to competition. Demand in the competitive business world will accordingly diminish. On the basis of a given social income, which determines the social demand, monopoly prices force other prices below what they would be under more perfect conditions of competition. What takes place here is a "transfer" of income from the more-competitive to the less-competitive businesses but not any kind of integrating social organization of production.

Such "transfers," however, need not affect the absolute size of any particular business-income under conditions of flux, that is, with a growing social income in an expanding market. Only under conditions of capital stagnation will the increasing monopolization, which, in part, is itself an expression of this stagnation, be accompanied by a progressive destruction of competitive enterprises, a process that would find its "logical" end in the complete monopolization of all business, which would also be the end of the capitalist market economy.

VI

The capitalist *stabilization, organization,* and *integration* of which Marcuse speaks is of a peculiar kind. In a paper presented to the *German Sociological Society,* in 1964, Marcuse describes "how mature capitalism, in the efficiency of its reason, makes even the planned annihilation of millions of human beings and the planned destruction of their labour the fountainhead of a bigger and better prosperity; even sheer insanity becomes the basis, not only of the continuation of life, but of a more comfortable life . . . In the face of inhuman misery and methodical cruelty, the 'affluent' society squanders its unimaginable technical, material, and intellectual power and uses it for the purpose of permanent mobilization."[30]

Obviously, the victims of this process could not possibly share such an enthusiasm for the "affluent society" as may be displayed by its profiteers. The situation itself splits society, and the oppositional forces deny Marcuse's concept of the one-dimensional society without opposition.

It is true, however, that the oppositional forces do not find expression in a class struggle between proletariat and bourgeoisie, but in capitalist competition, imperialistic rivalries, and the cold war between two dissimilar social systems. There are, then, many "one-dimensional" societies in conflict with one another. It is a situation that has prevailed for the last fifty years. These conflicts, if they denote anything, demonstrate the utter inability of capitalism to organize and stabilize an integrated capitalist world system able to dominate the foreseeable future.

Capitalism has always been simultaneously a productive and a destructive social system, not only in every-day competition, but, in an accelerated and concentrated form, in times of crisis and depression. Imperialist conflicts, finding their decisive source in economic rivalries, led to destructive world-wide wars. Both the destruction of capital values in peaceful competition and in competition by way of war were instrumental in bringing about a new upswing in capital production and a further extension of its markets. What Marcuse relates as typical for "mature capitalism," has been typical all along; only the social consequences were less devastating and less ferocious because the more limited possibilities of production also circumscribed those of destruction. The respective quantitative difference between the past and the present amounts to a qualitative difference in a twofold sense : not only does it include the technical possibility of destroying most of the world and its population but it excludes the utilization of war for purposes of capital accumulation.

In order to serve as instruments of accumulation, the destructive aspects of capital production must retain a certain definite relationship to its productive powers. The destruction of capital values in a depression affects only a small amount of capital in its physical form. The material productive apparatus remains largely intact and is merely concentrated into fewer hands in the form of lowered capital values. War, however, destroys capital in both its physical and its value form, and if too much is destroyed in its material form, the surviving capitals find themselves thrown back to an "earlier" stage of capital development in which their own advanced characteristics become an anachronism. Because their own profits are bound up with a definite mass of total social income, the reduction of the latter also reduces the profitability of the surviving capitals. In other terms, they cannot sell their products for lack of buyers because their own production and productivity demands a larger general production and productivity. The disproportionalities caused by the destruction and dislocations of war must first be overcome before the general process of capital accumulation can again proceed.

Two world wars failed to reinstate conditions of progressive private capital production such as existed in nineteenth-century capitalism. The last great depression on an international scale, which led to the Second World War, lasted too long and penetrated the social fabric too deeply to be still acceptable as a necessary evil for regaining the blessings of prosperity. Depressions of this nature seem no longer socially viable and thus must be prevented by government actions. They have lost their utility within the capital expansion process. And with regard to war as a medium of accumulation, it seems clear that a third world war between the capitalist powers would let loose such destructive forces as to destroy not only capitalism but society itself.

There is no future for capitalism in war and depression. Yet there are no other ways to effect the large-scale structural changes which the continuous expansion of capital production demands. To maintain the existing structure internationally, as well as in each capitalist nation separately, that is, to maintain the full employment of productive resources, now requires an increasing quantity of non-profitable production; in Marcuse's words, the "squandering of technical, material, and intellectual power for the purpose of permanent mobilization." To do so, and at the same time to maintain so-called affluency, productivity must be continuously increased to secure the necessary profitability of the relatively diminishing profit-producing part of the economy.

According to Marcuse, this is precisely what modern technology is accomplishing; it allows for both an unimaginable amount of waste-production and an "affluency," which, with the exception of a minority of unemployables, welds all social classes to the system and creates one-dimensional man. In this, Marcuse thinks, men are selling the prospects of a truly human, self-determined, future for the mess of pottage of today's high living standards. How much more worthwhile would their lives be, and how much better their standard of living, if waste-production were entirely eliminated and social production were rationally geared to the real needs of men.

Waste-production in an "affluent" society is, of course, what keeps that society "affluent," without, however, having the indirect effect of increasing the profitability of capital and its rate of accumulation. Profitability can only be maintained through increasing productivity, through labour-displacing and capital-saving technical innovations. The more "affluent" society becomes by means of waste-production, the greater is its need for labour-saving devices, so as to prevent the loss of profitability which

B*

would otherwise accompany the increase in production.

The steady increase in production and productivity through labour-saving devices has the twofold effect of increasing the profitability of capital and reproducing the need for further vast increases in productivity on an ever-narrowing base of capital production. Even if capital-saving innovations were to check the growing discrepancy between that capital invested in means of production and that invested in labour-power, and in this manner curb the fall of the rate of profit on total capital, this can only be a temporarily mitigating factor. The consistent displacement of labour must eventually terminate in the destruction of profitability and is, for that reason, an impossibility for capitalism. But neither can it do without the steady displacement of labour, for this is seemingly the only way left open to cope with the growing non-profitable production within the profit-producing economy. While the displacement of labour is a way out for capitalism, the way itself leads only into a *cul-de-sac*. What Marcuse considers a capitalistic solution to capitalism's difficulties, namely, its new technology, represents, instead, the present and future insoluble contradiction of capital production within the property relations of the market economy.

VII

Whereas future events may prove Marcuse right in his pessimism with respect to the chances of a working-class revolution, his "optimism" with regard to capitalism's ability to save itself by technological and political means will most probably be disproved by actual developments. At the present, of course, Marcuse's assertion can only be answered by a counter-assertion. In view of what has happened since the end of the second world war, it would appear that capitalism has found a way to escape the perils of its class structure, and has been able to transform itself in a society freed of effective opposition. Marcuse's "optimism" in this respect, it should be repeated, is not at all to his own liking; he accepts it only grudgingly in order to free himself of all illusions.

Any particular state of capitalism is transitory, even though it may prevail for a considerable length of time. But it is only by considering the general laws of capitalist development that any of its given historical situations reveal its transient nature. The future of capitalism rests on its continuing ability to extract sufficient profits out of social production to ensure its enlarged reproduction. A persistently declining rate of capital expansion indicates, increasingly, the loss of this ability, and this despite a general increase in production through government interventions. However, so long as the increase can still be conciliated with the decrease of private capital formation through the increasing productivity of labour, the "mixed economy" may be experienced not as a temporary possibility but as an actual transformation which resolves the contradictions of capital production. But this, too, is an illusion.

The question is then, can capitalism evolve into something other than it is; can the general laws of capitalist development be set aside by technological and political means, which attend to both the profit needs of private capital and the general welfare by the simple expediency of waste-production? It is true, that this is exactly what has happened. Yet to see this process as a permanent and ever-widening social practice is to assume that capitalism can transform itself into another system, in which—to speak in Marxian terms—it is no longer exchange-value but use-value that rules. Such a change would imply a change in property relations based, as they are, on the production and distribution of exchange-values. In other words, it would require a social revolution.

Not so, however, in Marcuse's opinion. The industrially-advanced society, he says, is "a static society, despite all its dynamism. Its non-stop expansion, its soaring productivity, its increasing growth produce nothing but more and more of the same, without any qualitative change or any hope of qualitative change."[31] But Marcuse also speaks of a capitalist "metamorphosis" in response to the phenomenon of the cold war, which first provides capitalism with the impetus to "organize" itself and to expand its production. Still, in his view, this "metamorphosis" implies not a qualitative but only a quantitative change, through "the ever-increasing tide of goods and the ever-increasing standard of living, which seem ever more desirable," and which provide the masses with "every reason to integrate themselves into the system."[32]

According to Marcuse, "even the most highly organized capitalism retains the social need for private appropriation and distribution of profit as the regulator of the economy."[33] It is for this reason that he dissociates himself from the position, held by some, that "the contemporary conflict between capitalism and communism is a conflict between two forms or modes of one and the same complex industrial society."[34] For him, there exists a fundamental difference between the nationalized and the private-enterprise economies, even though both systems share the same technology and the same inclination not to develop it in directions which would destroy the basis of class domination. Marcuse's "organized capitalism" is not identical with a state-regulated economy such as prevails in Russia, for, to repeat, it "retains the need for private appropriation and distribution of profit as the regulator of the economy."

If this is so, however, "organized capitalism" also retains capitalist value relations and it becomes necessary for Marcuse to demonstrate that these relations harmonize with the continuous expansion of production by technological and political means. In this connection, Marcuse quotes Marx to the effect that the machine never creates value but merely transfers its own value to the product, while surplus-value remains the result of the exploitation of living labour. The machine is the embodiment of human labour power, and through it, past labour (dead labour) preserves itself and determines living labour."[35] Considering automation, however, Marcuse remarks, that it "seems to alter qualitatively the relation between dead and living labour; it tends toward the point where productivity is determined by the machines, and not by the individual output."[36] This also occurred to Marx, who pointed out that social wealth is not only a value relation but is embodied, in increasing measure, in a productive apparatus which turns the productivity of labour into the productivity of capital. Although the means of production represent a definite sum of values and can

capitalistically be productive only through the enlargement of this sum of values, in their real, physical
form, and by their continuous development, it is the
quantity and quality of the means of production,
not labour-time, which expresses the growing productive powers of social labour. For Marx, "labour-
time ceases to be the measure of wealth, and exchange-
value ceases to be the measure of use-value, as soon
as labour in its direct form ceases to be the source of
wealth."[37]

But for Marx, the abolition of value relations is
the abolition of capitalism itself. If it were not for
capitalist relations of production, the growing social
wealth would be characterized by a continuous
reduction of direct labour time, and the wealth of
society would be measured not by labour time but by
free time. So long, however, as exchange-value is the
goal of production, labour-time quantities remain
the source and measure of capitalist wealth, because,
as value, capital cannot be anything other than
appropriated labour-time. "Although the very development of the modern means of production," Marx
wrote, "indicates to what a large degree the general
knowledge of society has become a direct productive
power, which conditions the social life and determines its transformation,"[38] capitalism's particular
contribution to this state of affairs consists of no more
"than in its use of all the media of the arts and
sciences to increase the surplus-labour, because its

wealth, in value form, is nothing but the appropriation of surplus-labour time."[39]

The diminution of labour as the source and measure of value already takes place under capitalist conditions. Depending on actual conditions and the structure of capital, it may have either a positive or a negative effect upon the accumulation of capital. Now, when Marcuse says, "that even the most highly organized capitalism retains the social need for private appropriation and distribution of profit as the regulator of the economy," he is saying only that the value relations of capital production are here retained and regulate the economy. In other words, the economy is "regulated" by its ability or inability to produce surplus-value, and not by its ability or inability just to produce. The private appropriation and distribution of profit presupposes market relations, and these market relations presuppose value relation. Under these conditions, profit remains surplus-value, or surplus-labour, even where the relations between "dead" and "living" labour have been reversed. And under these conditions, the diminution of labour relative to the growing mass of capital implies a reduction of surplus-value, except where the productivity of labour increases at a faster pace than the quantity of labour diminishes.

It is the productivity of labour, not the "productivity of capital", which accounts for the capitalist profit. To be sure, profit presupposes the existence of capital, and the more "productive" this capital is in its physical form, the higher the profits may rise. Still, profits can only be the difference between paid and unpaid labour. If, in some mysterious way, they should derive from the "productivity of capital," independently of the labour which first sets this capital in motion, they would not be profits in the capitalistic sense, that is, the result of labour exploitation. It would still be true that capital represents transformed past surplus-labour, but it would no longer determine living labour. Actually, of course, capital presupposes wage-labour just as wage-labour presupposes capital; both are the two necessary sides of the capitalist production relations for the production of surplus-value. Where there is no capital involved in production, there is no capitalist society, and where capital is no longer dependent on wage-labour, capitalism has ceased to exist.

Marcuse himself points out that "automation, once it becomes *the* process of material production, would revolutionize the whole society."[40] It is for this reason, he says, that both the nationalized and the private-enterprise economies must contain technological development and "arrest material and intellectual growth at a point where domination still is rational and profitable."[41] In his view, however, this point seems to be far off, and, meanwhile capitalism responds to the "challenge of communism by a spectacular development of all productive forces after the subordination of private interests in profitability which arrest such development."[42]

Moreover, according to Marcuse, it is not only the "challenge of communism" which brings this change about, but also the "technological process and mass production, which shatter the individualistic forms in which progress operated during the liberalistic era."[43] Apart from the fact that these "individualistic forms" were first decisively shattered in technologically-backward nations without mass production, were it actually true that these "individualistic forms" are shattered, it could not simultaneously be true that "private appropriation and distribution of profit" is being retained as the "regulator of the economy", nor could it be true that "private interests in profitability" have been "subordinated" to the social need of a further "spectacular advance of the productive forces."

One cannot have it both ways; either the economy is left to its "self-regulation" via the value-price relations in a competitive market of individually-oriented producers, that is, capitalistically; or it is consciously regulated, more or less successfully, by government decisions considering the national economy as a whole on the basis of its particular institutional arrangements. A combination of market- and planned-regulation of the economy can only be a side-by-side affair; it does not really "mix" the economy, but tends, in the course of development, to eliminate one side or the other, unless one of these sides can always be held in a subordinate position. But to hold it there is to limit its effectiveness.

VIII

We must here recapitulate. In order to sustain the capitalistic character of the economy, government-induced production must be non-competitive with private capital. If it were otherwise it would, in the course of time, supplant private production. This being so, the expanding government-induced production cannot enhance but can only hem in private capital formation, for its expenses must ultimately be carried by the private sector of the economy. The maintenance of private capital production thus sets a definite limit to the enlargement of government-induced production. Consequently, the continuous expansion of production must be attained by private production. But this private production is subject to value relations and their market appearance and finds its limits in its own expansion. There are, then, within the capitalist relations of production, limits set to both private production and government-induced production; the limits of the latter are the limits of capital production itself.

The "mixed" character of present-day capitalism is only apparent, due to the fact that government-induced production stimulates the whole of the economy. It is obvious that public works and waste-production employs machinery, materials, and labour. The money invested in these items is spent in the private sector of the economy and to that extent increases the private market demand. But—still to recapitulate—the money itself stems from the private sector of the economy, which turns the whole process into an extension of the credit mechanism. Private capital could—and to some extent does—do so of its own accord. It does not do so extensively enough, because, in the light of existing market conditions, the expansion of production is clearly not credit-worthy. While private capital hesitates, the government guarantees a further credit expansion by directing it into non-competitive production. Nevertheless, production is thereby generally increased, as the government's initiative creates additional markets for all the capitals involved in producing goods that enter into government-induced production, including the consumption goods of the labourers employed therein. The *final product* of government-induced production, resulting from a long chain of intermediary production processes, however, does not have the form of a commodity which could profitably be sold on the market. Whatever entered into its production were its production-costs, which cannot be recovered in a sales price, for there are no buyers of public works and waste-products.

The dual-economy, with its public and private sector, will thus appear as a "mixed" economy benefiting both private capital and society at large. It will be celebrated, or deplored, as a new type of capitalism, even as a "post-capitalist" system—as it has already been called by some people. Yet, it is still the familiar capitalism, held together by government interventions which, by their own nature, and the nature of capitalism, can only be of temporary avail. While solving some problems immediately, these interventions open up new and larger problems in the foreseeable future.

When evaluating the state of the economy, economists do not usually distinguish between government-induced and private-capital production. Although each goes its separate way, in that the one is profitable and the other not, they are nevertheless inseparably intertwined in the actual production and marketing process. For all *practical* reasons, then the economy is a "mixed economy," even though government-induced production cannot add but only subtract from the total profit of total social production. Nonetheless, government-induced production is usually regarded as a medium of capital formation. But this view merely mistakes the postponement of a problem for its disappearance.

While a vast increase in productivity enables the simultaneous growth of private and government productions, the resulting prosperity is quite deceptive, as it is based, by way of the credit mechanism, on future profits which may, or may not, materialize. Moreover, just as the prosperity itself is based on a continuous and accelerating increase in productivity so is its continuation. This requires the displacement of less-productive by more-productive means of production, and therewith the transformation of part of the realizable profit into additional capital. It is in this fashion that a need for always larger profits accompanies the prolongation of prosperity.

While, however, on the one hand, the "productivity of capital" increases through its modernization because it allows for a higher productivity of labour, on the other hand, "the productivity of labour" declines because of the higher productivity of capital. This is not as paradoxical as it sounds. In capitalism, "productivity of labour" always refers to the production of profits. The increase in the "productivity of capital" implies that new capital is added to existing capital. The new and the old capital constitute an entity, a certain quantity of value, expressed in money terms. To avoid disinvestment, the whole capital must be reproduced and enlarged. The larger, modernized capital implies a shift in investment relations; a relatively larger amount of capital is now invested in means of production than in labour power. But the modernization allows fewer workers to produce more, and this raises the rate of profit despite the decline of applied labour-power. Still, there are fewer workers and a larger capital, and the process which brought it about must be repeated over and over again.

We will not go into the technical details of why the profit-reducing effect of a declining number of workers cannot perpetually be neutralized, or over-compensated for, by their increasing productivity, and why, for that reason, the tendency of a falling rate of profit must turn into its actual decline at a certain stage of capital expansion. For, in view of the present threat of automation, it is now almost generally discerned, however vaguely, that the growing discrepancy between labour and capital must come to a point which would exclude a further progressive capital expansion through labour exploitation.

This growing conviction implies an unconscious acceptance of Marx's theory of accumulation, if only because it is dressed in non-Marxian terms. Instead of deducing the eventual collapse of capitalism from the "productivity of labour," which is only another expression for the accumulation of capital, the inverted "Marxists" deduce it from the "productivity of capital" and its tendency to displace labour. In either case, the system of capital production through labour exploitation comes to an end. Since the growing productivity of labour implies the growing productivity of capital, and *vice versa,* the end of capitalism by way of automation equates with the end of capitalism for lack of surplus-value.

But whatever the theory, the end of capitalism seems far away, because surplus-value is still produced in sufficient measure to secure the profitability of capital within the conditions of a declining rate of capital expansion, and automation, considered in relation to world-capitalism, is as yet no more than an exotic exception to a rather stagnant technology.

We will recall that Marx's accumulation theory operates on a high level of abstraction, which only considers the essentials of the capital-labour relations in a mental construction, or model, which is not a replica of reality. The developmental tendencies inherent in these basic relationships are continuously either precipitated or countermanded by actual occurrences in the real world of capitalism. But, unless adjudged in the light of the abstract theory, the concrete conditions would not be understandable, nor would they offer a clue to the actual development. To make statements regarding the actual course of events, however, it is the events themselves, not the theory which elucidates their meaning, that are of foremost importance. This is true for any other theory and also for that which sees technology as the essential element in the total process of social evolution. The question is then not what automation could do, but what it actually is doing under given conditions, and what the conditions would have to be for its unhindered development.

According to Marcuse, automation, which "would turn work-time into fringe-time and free-time into full-time . . . cannot be realized within the (existing) political and economic institutions; . . . it would mean, plainly, the final catastrophe of the capitalist system."[44] In saying this, Marcuse refutes, at least to some extent, another, simultaneously-held position, namely, that modern technology "transcends" the capitalist mode of production. But what is new in technology is just this automation business, which, if inapplicable in capitalism, means that this mode of production also "transcends" technology, that is, determines the degree of its development. To be sure, there is quite a difference between full automation and partial automation, but why it can only be partial and not full, depends again on the mode of production.

Transcendance means for Marcuse to "overshoot the established universe of discourse and action towards its historical alternative."[45] Automation is seen as the alternative to capitalism, for which reason it cannot be realized in capitalism. Since it appears, nonetheless, in capitalism, it should, to that extent, indicate the beginning of the end of capitalism and not its "stabilization" and "integration." Marcuse assumes, however, that capitalism is able to use the new technology, including partial automation, to secure its own existence simply by raising living standards and by an enormous increase in waste-production. Sooner or later, however, the system would still be forced to arrest further technical development in the direction of automation, for the number of unemployables would come to exceed that of the employed. Eventually, a small minority would have to provide for the large majority, thus reversing the usual conditions of class society. But where and when to stop this process—since any of its ascending stages brings the dissolution of the capitalist system so much nearer?

In so far as technology transcends the capitalist system of production, it points towards another social system. According to Marx, the developing social forces of production which grow with, but cannot be accommodated within, the capitalist relations of production constitute a social contradiction to be resolved by way of social transformation. In Marcuse's view, which excludes a social revolution, the transcending technology dominates society by adapting its social relations to the technology. It does not really point to a historical alternative, but issues into "the progressive enslavement of man by a productive apparatus which perpetuates the struggle for existence."[46] Despite acknowledged differences between the nationalized and the private-enterprise economies,

Marcuse fears, for instance, that the incorporation of capitalist technology into socialism will show there the same evil effects as it does in capitalism. Because of this, he speculates "about the possible assimilation of the two systems."[47] The main villain is, then, not capitalism but science and technology, for it threatens to, or does already, nullify the effects of a social transformation from capitalism to socialism.

IX

It is rather strange to find Marcuse following the general pattern in using the terms *socialism* and *communism* when referring to a society such as exists in Russia. As for "ideological communism," and for the bourgeoisie proper, for Marcuse, too, nationalization creates "the socialist base of production." For Marcuse, however, "nationalization, without initiative and control 'from below' by the 'immediate producer', is but a technological-political device for increasing the productivity of labour, for accelerating the development of the productive forces and for their control from above—a change in the mode of domination, rather than prerequisite for its abolition."[48] In his view, it is thus only a half-truth that the class relations of private property society are no longer the motor of the nationalized production process; "the other half of the truth is that quantitative change would still have to turn into qualitative change, into the disappearance of the State, the Party, the Plan, etc., as independent powers superimposed on the individuals."[49] But in as much "as this change would leave the material base of society (the nationalized productive process) intact, it would be confined to a political revolution."[50] Unfortunately, however, Marcuse remarks that "the ruled tend not only to submit to the rulers but also to reproduce in themselves their subordination. This process is not specific to Soviet Society. The means and rewards of highly advanced industrial society, the work and leisure attitudes called forth by its organization of production and distribution, establish a human existence which makes for a change in basic values —for a transformation of freedom into security."[51]

What Marx failed to foresee, to come back to a previously-raised point, was not the general course of technological development but the possibility of the nationalization of production as a new form of capitalization and exploitation. To be sure, he also spoke of the nationalization of the means of production, but only as a once-undertaken revolutionary act and prelude to the institution of socialism. For

Marx, capitalism was private-property capitalism, and where it seemed to lose its strictly private-enterprise nature, as in state-industries, and even in the joint stock companies, he saw it as a partial abolition of the capitalist mode of production within the capitalist mode of production; a sign of the decay of the capitalist system. He did not contemplate systems of state-capitalism such as prevail in the so-called socialist part of the world. For him, moreover, only highly-developed capitalist nations contained the pre-conditions for socialism; the over-accumulation of capital, not its underdeveloped status, caused those particular social frictions which were expected to lead to socialist revolutions.

But aside from Marx's "failure of prediction," it is not the adoption of the capitalist technology by the so-called socialist regimes which may prevent them from turning the "half-truth" of their designation as socialist states into the "full-truth" of socialist freedom. It is their shift from private- to state-appropriation of surplus-labour which turns the apparent "half-truth" into a full lie. It is a social transformation, not technology, which accounts for the deplorable conditions in the nominally socialist nations. Not other "values," but another social transformation is called for, since the change from private- to state-control of the means of production has proved not to be a "base of socialist production."

It is a base for the production of capital and

therefore for the reproduction of wage-labour, which does not allow a choice between "freedom and security," but, in fact, excludes both. Still, nationalized capital is the opposite of private capital, even though —as regards the producers—both forms of capital production thrive on exploitation. This is the point of their "assimilation," while they remain divided on all other issues. It is this common point which encourages the current hope for their eventual convergence. But while both systems agree on the importance of capital production, they disagree on the far more important question as to what particular social layers are to be its beneficiaries. ᐧWhile in the "Soviet" system war and revolution decided the issue to the detriment of private capital, it still agitates the "Western" system as an opposition to internal socialization and to the "communist" world. In view of the complete absence of a socialist opposition, the capitalist opposition to "socialism" restricts itself to being opposed to an extension of government controls which would endanger and eventually destroy the private-enterprise character of the economy.

The nationalized economy is no longer a market economy, even though it may retain, or re-introduce, some quasi-market relations subordinated to overall government control. Good or bad, it can actually plan its production and distribution, although the nature of the planning itself is co-determined by internal necessities, the world market, and the changing requirements of the cold-war situation. It can plan the avoidance of exploitation by capitalist nations, if not always in trade relations, at any rate, with respect to foreign investments. In this way, it sets borders to the extension of private capital production. Its own existence and extension in space endangers the existence of private capitalism by limiting the latter's expansion. To secure the continuing existence of the private-enterprise system it is therefore essential to contain the spreading of nationalized production and, if possible, to put an end to it altogether.

The strictness of the opposition between private and government control over the means of production, between the market and the regulated capitalist economy, seems to be contradicted by the existence of the "mixed economy" and its projection onto the international scene as a possible harmonious co-existence of different social systems. Of course, a strictly capitalist private enterprise economy never and nowhere existed; the private sector was always accompanied by a public sector, which varied in its relative importance according to specific historical conditions of the developing capitalist nations. But the public sector was regarded not as an independent sector of the economy, but as an unavoidable expense for assuring the proper functioning of the market economy. This was no less so, even where the public sector includes—besides the military capital—the transportation system, utilities, and other special industries. All in all, whether more or less extensive, the public sector always did account for the smaller part of the national economy.

The governments of "mixed economies" restrict their economic activities to non-productive, that is, non-profitable endeavours, as, in the United States, for instance, in nuclear and space technology, which have no conceivable application in other fields and cannot directly find commercial exploitation. Or they enter deficit-industries, such as coal mining in England and France, which can no longer be profitably operated and expanded by private capital, but can continue to function when backed by the public purse. Governments may also enter the private sphere of commodity production by the capitalization of under-capitalized industries with public funds as in Norway, for example, and in this manner increase their competitive abilities to the advantage of both government and private enterprise. Or industries may be nationalized for political reasons, as happened in France after the Second World War to punish certain French firms which had collaborated with the enemy.

In whatever manner, and for whatever reason capitalist governments may enter the sphere of production, they do so to support, not to destroy, private capital production. In theory, of course, it could be otherwise. In a "democracy," it is not entirely inconceivable that a government may come to power committed to the slow or rapid nationalization of industry. Such a government would be a revolutionary, anti-capitalist government, in so far as capitalism is identified with private ownership of the means of production. In order to realize its programme, it would be forced to displace the market system by a planning system, so as to enable itself centrally to allocate productive resources and to organize production and distribution on a non-competitive basis. As far as the capitalists are concerned, it would be their death-warrant, and it is not easily conceivable that they would accept it without protest. Most likely, the nationalization of industry would lead to civil war. It is fear of the social consequences of an extensive nationalization which prevents those ideologically committed to it from actually attempting its realization. "Labour governments" in England and elsewhere never utilize their governmental power to advance nationalization beyond the point where it could no longer be tolerated by private capital.

X

Short of social revolution, it is highly improbable that the market economy would slowly transform itself into a planned economy. It is equally improbable that a once-nationalized economy would return to capitalist market relations. The restoration of the market would mean the restoration of private capital, if not *de jure,* at any rate, *de facto.* In the Western capitalist nations there exists the false concept of a "peoples' capitalism," i.e., a system wherein stock-ownership is widely dispersed and where, in consequence, there arises a division between the ownership and the control of capital. What interests us here is only the alleged divorce between ownership and control, which seemingly turns the non-owning managers of industry into acting capitalists. If the functions of the capitalists can be exercised by management without ownership, the rewards of ownership may also become the rewards of management. Although hardly probable, it is not inconceivable that the managers of Russian industry, in collaboration with the government, and with the consent of large layers of the population, might proceed to restore a competitive market economy based on private profit production, in the sense that each enterprise would operate as any private entrepreneur, or corporation, would. As before, government would siphon off the equivalent of its own requirements from both paid and unpaid labour by way of taxes. But this would constitute a private-capitalist counter-revolution under the guise of a "managerial revolution," and would at once reintroduce into the Russian economy all the contradictions which are immanent in competitive private capital production.

What a private-enterprise economy can engage in, short of social revolution, is a form of pseudo-planning, and what the nationalized economy can restore, short of social counter-revolution, is some sort of pseudo-market. In either case, the spurious market competition, or the spurious planning attempt, indicate existing difficulties within the market system or within the planned economy. But to combat these difficulties with instrumentalities foreign to the respective systems and their specific needs, while, perhaps, of some temporary usefulness, will have to be arrested in time to secure the systems' basic characteristics. There is no congruency between the planned and the market system, even though some economic-technical arrangements, in distinction to social-economic relations, may be common to both.

All the state-capitalist, or, if one prefers, state-socialist, systems resemble the capitalist market economy in their maintenance of capital-labour relations and their adaptations of capitalistic business methods. Instead of being owned by capitalists, the means of production are now controlled by governments. The latter set a certain value (in money terms) upon productive resources and expect a greater value (in money terms) through the intermediary of production. Money wages are paid to the workers, whose function it is to create a greater value than that represented by their wages. The surplus is allocated in accordance with the decisions of government. It feeds the non-working layers of society, secures national defence, takes care of public requirements, and is re-invested in additional capital. All economic transactions are either exchange transactions, or appear as such. Labour-power is sold to management of some enterprises and wages buy commodities from management of other enterprises. There is quasi-trade between the management of some enterprises and the management of other enterprises, such as is carried on between the various divisions of large corporations in all capitalist nations, and which reaches its complete form in the fully centralized state economy. *Formally,* there is not much difference between private-enterprise economy and state-controlled economy, except the *centralized control over the surplus-product,* or surplus-value.

All actually-existing state-controlled systems were, or are, to be found in capital-poor nations. Their first requirement is the formation of capital as a pre-supposition for their national independence and as precondition for the intended socialization of production and distribution. Bound more or less (depending on the country and its particular situation) to the capitalistic "international division of labour," they must relate their economies to world market conditions, and must partake in international commercial competition, which limits or excludes a possible desire on their part not to make the money-economy and its expansion the motive force of their activities. The emphasis is on accumulation and therewith on exploitation—which also characterizes the capitalist economy.

The "socialization" of the means of production is here still only the *nationalization of capital as capital,* i.e., though private ownership no longer exists, the means of production have still the character of capital by being controlled by government instead of being at the disposal of the whole of society. Although private capital accumulation is now excluded, the exploitation of men by men continues by way of an unequal system of distribution with respect to both the conditions of production and the conditions of consumption. This perpetuates competition as a struggle for lucrative positions and better-paid jobs, and carries the antagonisms of capitalism into the state-capitalist system.

State-capitalism is still a surplus-labour producing system, but it is no longer a system which finds its "regulation" through market competition and crisis. The surplus-product no longer requires competition in order to be realized as profit; it derives its specific material character, and its distribution, from conscious decisions on the part of the state's planning agencies. That these decisions are co-determined by international economic and political competition and by the requirements of accumulation does not change the fact that the lack of an *internal capital market* demands a centrally-determined direct system of decision-making with regard to the allocation of the total social labour and the distribution of the total social product.

Under these conditions, the use of quasi-market relations is a convenience, so to speak, not a necessity, even though it may have been forced upon the state-capitalist systems by circumstances they were unwilling to resist. In the U.S.S.R., for example, the quasi-market relations provide enterprises with a quasi-autonomy, the consumers with a quasi-freedom of choice of consumption, and the workers with a quasi-choice of occupation. But all these quasi-market relations are subordinated to over-all direction by government.

Within definite limits, this restricted "free play" of market forces can be extended or contracted without seriously affecting the planning system as such. Presently, it is extended in the belief that this will make for greater "efficiency," without diminishing the effectiveness of the planning system. It involves some de-centralization of the decision-making process and more self-determination for individual enterprises—not in opposition to, but in support of, the overall direction of the economy as a whole. The goal is not to change the character of the economy, but merely to provide it with a greater profitability through a more extensive use of capitalistic incentives.

Individual enterprises are given more leeway in determining their production processes, so as to fulfill and excel their planned production quotas; a greater regard for consumers' preferences is expected to aid production plans and to eliminate waste; interest charges on borrowed capital are supposed to lead to greater economic rationality in investment decisions; wage differences within the plant are left to some extent to the discretion of management; portions of the profits made through higher productivity and improved organization may be retained by management and reflected in wage increases. These and other "innovations" are intended to *accentuate* what has always existed, namely, the use of capitalistic incentives in state-capitalist economy. They do not affect the control of investments by government, nor,

to that end, the control of total social production and
its division in accordance with a general plan. Where-
ever the outcome of these "innovations" does not
suit the general plan, a government veto can change
the situation either by decree or through a change in
pricing policies. The limited "free market" can at any
time be suspended by the real power relations behind
the pseudo-market relations.

It should be obvious in any case that at a time when
not even the private-enterprise system is able to exist
except through extensive government interventions,
no state-capitalist system will find itself on the road
of return to the private-enterprise system. In fact, its
only advantage over the latter consists of its complete
control over economic affairs, to compensate for its
economic ineffectiveness vis-a-vis the highly-developed
private-capitalist systems. The state-capitalist system
does not suffer that particular contradiction between
profitable   and   non-profitable   production   which
plagues private-property capitalism, and which offers
as an alternative to stagnation only its destruction as
a private-enterprise economy. Having this destruction
already behind itself, the state-capitalist economy
may also produce profitably and non-profitably, but
this need not lead to stagnation.

Not to digress any further, we will merely empha-
size that an indefinite peaceful co-existence of state-
capitalist and market-oriented economies is no less
illusory than the indefinite existence of the "mixed

economy" as a market-economy. In fact, it is precisely the advancing state-control in the private-enterprise economies which accentuates the conflict between the two different capitalistic systems. The wars between identical capitalist systems have made it clear that capital competition turns into imperialistic competition and that wars would occur even if there were not a single state-capitalist nation. The Second World War demonstrated the feasibility of temporary alliances between state-capitalist and "liberalistic" systems of capital production; but, at the same time, it also demonstrated the basic irreconcilability of these two systems, not merely because of newly-arising conflicting national and imperialistic interests but also because of their different social structures. Far from bringing "traditional" capitalism closer to state-controlled economies, the advent of the "mixed economy" intensifies their enmities, if only to curtail the expansion of state-control in the market economies. In current political terms, the "containment of communism" becomes a pre-condition for the continuing existence of the private-enterprise system.

XI

Marcuse sees the factor of co-existence as both a divisive and a unifying force. It is competition which, in his view, distorts but also "benefits" both systems; it explains the rapid development of "communism" as well as the unleashed productivity of capitalism. It explains, too, the unsavoury aspects of both systems. For instance, Marcuse thinks that "the situation of hostile co-existence may explain the terroristic features of Stalinist industrialization."[52] However, all capitalistic existence is hostile co-existence. Terrorism, moreover, was not confined to Stalin's Russia, nor did it find its roots there so much in hostile co-existence as in the transformation of the Russian peasant-economy into state-controlled economy. In so far as the terror had a "rational" ground, it was the incongruity between centralistic planning and market production which induced the Stalinist regime to destroy the budding private-capitalist system through the destruction of peasant farming and small-scale industry. This is not to deny that Russia's forced industrialization was necessary to secure the existence of the Bolshevik regime. But it was not hostile co-existence which led to the distortion of "socialism"; terror was used to end the co-existence with the potential "internal enemy," that is, with the private-capitalist tendencies inherent in peasant production, which threatened to undo the state-capitalist character of the Bolshevik revolution. Neither does co-existence explain the apparent consolidation of capitalism, to enable one to say, as Marcuse feels inclined to do, that "communism has become the doctor by the sickbed of capitalism." If it were not for communism, he says, "it would be impossible to explain the political and economic unification of the capitalist world."[53]

The political and economic unification of the capitalist world of which Marcuse speaks, does not really exist. Marcuse himself recognizes that "there are still numerous contradictions among the imperialist powers but," in his view, "these contradictions no longer seem likely to lead, in the foreseeable future, to the outbreak of war."[54] But the unlikelihood of war among the capitalist powers—by itself—does not make for political and economic unification of the capitalist world. It was war itself, in fact, which led to that degree of "unification" of which the capitalist world is capable, namely, the combination of some nations against a combination of other nations. Under present conditions, as pointed out before, war no longer offers a way out for capitalism. But this does not mean that capitalism will not resort to war, or that war will not overwhelm capitalism. In fact, the small-scale wars presently waged may be seen as the harbingers of new world-wide conflagrations which, as such, may explain what measure of capitalistic unity still endures.

The only "unification" of which capitalism is capable, and which amounts to more than a temporary alliance for waging war, is unification by way of absorption, through the national and international concentration and centralization of capital. On the international scale, this requires a "free" world market and the "free" movement of capital; in other words nineteenth-century conditions such as allowed for some degree of capitalistic integration in economic terms. This "unity" by way of market relations is irretrievably lost. Economic integration must now be brought about by political means, by government activities, through alliances, which set groups of nations against other groups of nations. A real economic fusion of the capitalist world would imply the sacrifice of the profitability principle in favour of a rational allocation of the productive resources according to national needs; in brief, it would imply the abolition of capitalism. Short of this, "integration" can only mean the creation of spheres of interests, of economic blocs, opposed to other economic blocs. But the creation of such blocs attests to no more than an intensified capital competition in a shrinking world market. And even these limited forms of capitalist "unification" necessitate conditions of prosperity. Under crisis conditions they fall apart again as each nation seeks to extricate itself at the expense of other nations.

Designed and built-up with a view towards an expanding world market, the productive apparatus in the capitalistically-advanced countries exceeds the scope of their national markets. As this is more or less true for all capitalist nations, their combined production exceeds the scope of the world market, unless this world market should expand as fast as industrial production. In the past it proved more profitable for Western capitalism to restrict industrial development to its own part of the world. Once this monopolistic position was reached and consolidated, it could not freely be given up without seriously disturbing the whole fabric of Western capitalism. To preserve the non-industrial countries as markets for the manufacturing industries of the industrial nations was then the commercial policy of all developed nations, and was politically enforced in countries under their control. Quite aside from the question as to whether or not the underdeveloped countries, if they had been left alone, would have initiated industrial development on their own, the presence and dominance of the colonial powers were hindrance enough and subjected whatever development there was to their own needs. Nature itself, it was asserted, destined

some countries to be producers of industrial commodities and others to be producers of primary
products. More than a "natural fact", it was also an
economic convenience, as elucidated by the theory
of comparative costs, i.e., the notion that it was more
"economical" to produce primary products in
primary-goods producing countries as well as more
"economical" to produce industrial commodities in
industrial nations. In this way, supposedly, everyone
gained by the "international division of labour", that
is, by the division of the world into industrial and
non-industrial nations. Actually, however, the exchange between these countries was always advan-
tageous to the developed ones and dis-advantageous
to the underdeveloped.

The enrichment of the capitalist world was the
impoverishment of the non-capitalist world. Because
of the colonial and semi-colonial character of the
underdeveloped countries, attempts on their part to
escape the debilitating situations of an "international
division of labour" determined by, and favouring,
the capitalization needs of the industrially-advanced
nations requires political struggles, leading to some
degree of national independence, which assures a
national development different from that decided
by the market-determined "self-expansion" of capital. In so far as it was possible at all, their capitalistic
transformation appears then as a national development, and often as a national-revolutionary develop-

ment. This is, of course, a very complex process, involving social movements and national ideologies; and to be successful, it requires favourable conditions such as grow out of the disruptions of world economy through crises and wars.

Whereas the nationalism of the last century extended the "free world market" and that degree of economic "interdependency" possible under conditions of private capital formation—in spite of all the protectionism which was tactically employed—present-day nationalism arose in opposition to the results of private capital accumulation on a "free world market." The capitalization of the underdeveloped part of the world proceeds in opposition to the Western capital monopoly, since the latter is neither willing nor able to capitalize the world. Capital movements are governed by profitability and, more recently, by considerations of security. The most profitable economies attract most of the world's capital and increase their productivity accordingly. This diminishes continually the already precarious competitive ability of less-productive, under-capitalized nations, and assures their intensified exploitation under existing international market relations. Poor in capital, they are destined to become poorer in every respect through the constant widening of the productivity-gap between the developed and the underdeveloped nations.

Most of the underdeveloped nations do not have

an industry able to grow and prosper through protection from foreign competition. Such industry has first to be created. But the extraction of surplus-labour for the required capital development out of a large and predominantly peasant population—already close to the starvation level—is, if possible at all, a long-drawn-out, gruesome undertaking requiring the work of generations. It has been attempted, nevertheless, under more or less favourable conditions. But it necessitates the elimination of foreign exploitation and the over-all control of the national economy so that industrial development will have priority over private interests. This brings these economies in deadly conflict not only with their own traditional ruling classes, operating, as they do, within the conditions of the capitalist world market, but also with the market-determined structure of world capitalism.

Not only do the concentration and centralization tendencies immanent in competitive capital production impede the industrialization of world production, in time, and because of the increasing pauperization of the underdeveloped areas of the world; they also delimit the expansion of the concentrated capital in the advanced nations. By fostering only the exploitation of primary goods, by transferring profits made in these areas to the industrially-advanced nations, and by way of terms of trade favouring the developed capitalist countries, the underdeveloped areas' ability to buy manufactured goods is progressively reduced. The poorer the underdeveloped nations become, the less they offer a market for the products of the industrially-advanced countries. The more they deliver to the capitalist world, the less they receive from it, and the less able they are to capitalize themselves and to increase with the general demand also the demand for goods from the developed nations.

The state of the underdeveloped part of the world testifies to capitalism's inability to extend its mode of production into a world system. All it was able to do was to create the world market, and it was this creation itself which divided the world into "poor" and "rich" nations. The amassing of capital to private account disregards all real social needs, nationally and internationally, yet by doing so, capital production comes into always sharper conflict with the actual requirements of the world population. It also destroys its markets at a time when, in view of its increased productivity and production, it should extend them more than ever before; but this is only an indication that market relations are now completely out of any kind of harmony with the productive forces released by capitalism, or, what is the same thing, capitalist property relations have become an obstacle to a further expansion of the social forces of production on a world-wide scale.

The production of surplus-labour, or profit, which

is itself diminishing because of the structural changes in the capital-labour relations, is only half, though the basic half, of the difficulties in the way of capital expansion. The other half concerns the problem of profit realization, the need, that is, to sell the produced commodities at prices guaranteeing the profitability of capital. The increase in production through increasing productivity must lead to the extension of markets, for otherwise capital will not only be unprofitable but would in part be lost.

From the point of view of a single capital, an increase of productivity, and even automation, is no doubt a good thing, if this capital is thereby enabled to enlarge its market through the elimination of less-efficient competitors. What it loses in the production of profits because of the decrease of surplus-labour, so to speak, it regains and exceeds through the enlargement of its market. To be sure, the individual capital is not aware, nor could it be aware, of the loss of profit through the loss of surplus-labour, as its only considerations are its production costs and its returns on sales. The decline in surplus-labour shows itself only socially as the decline in the average rate of profit on total capital, which is merely an additional reason for each capital to maintain its own profitability through the expansion of its capital.

It is in this fashion that the decline of profitability accentuates the search for greater productivity and therewith the search for new markets. As this is a world of many nations, the process going on in each nation separately is repeated on the international scale, which is to say, that the capital concentration process finds an international extension. Just as in a single nation the more efficient capitals usurp a larger market at the expense of less-efficient capitals, so the more productive nations attempt to increase their shares of the world market at the expense of other nations. It implies the destruction of weaker capitals abroad just as it implies their destruction at home. Only abroad it is more difficult; nations resist the encroachments of other capitalist nations. Competition is both economic and political and in state-capitalist countries its political form takes precedence.

At a time when the further concentration of capital and the further increase in productivity in the highly-advanced capitalist nations are yielding diminishing returns, these nations look more intently to the outside world for profits and markets which will secure their solvency—not to speak of their expansion requirements. But the horizon of capital production and its realization narrows for the "free" market economies as industry begins to develop in hitherto raw-material producing areas, and as the rise of a "second world market"—dominated and controlled by the newly-developing state-capitalist systems—shrinks the capitalist world market of old. As the new system spreads, opportunities for the old contract, and this at a time when it must expand to secure a future for the

private-enterprise economy. Capitalistic world politics consists then in keeping open the closing world
of private profit production, if necessary by the
physical destruction of state-capitalist nations. The
"defence" of the "free world" is the defence of a
particular system of profit production which rightly
feels itself threatened by the results of its own history.

The present world situation as well as the conditions in the separate capitalist nations are not
as Marcuse believes, characterized by stabilization,
organization, and integration. On the contrary, the
capitalist world is far more unstable, disorganized,
and disintegrated than it was, say, fifty years ago.
The current mixture of free *and* controlled production, of free *and* controlled market relations, instead
of making for greater order, exclude both an "auto-
matic" and a "controlled" integration of both the
national and the world economy. Moreover, nationalism as imperialism, and nationalism in opposition to
imperialism lead to an always greater international
decomposition at a time when the actual world conditions and the physical production processes are in
need of the closest economic integration so as to
satisfy the most immediate requirements of the world
population.

XII

Capitalism has long ceased to be a socially-progressive system of production and has become—notwithstanding all the superficial appearances to the contrary—a regressive and destructive form of social production. It has led to the division of the world into a few highly-industrialized countries and a large number of nations unable to lift themselves out of a state of increasing poverty. Yet the destinies of all nations are inextricably intertwined; it is the situation as a whole, the world situation, which finally determines the future of any and all nations. The prospects for even the most prosperous countries must be considered in the light of existing world conditions, and seen in this way they are indeed bleak. The conditions for prosperity form rather small cases in a huge desert of human misery.

No longer able to extract out of their own working populations the quantities of surplus-labour that would secure a profitable private capital accumulation, the dominating capitalist powers find that the sources of surplus-labour in the underdeveloped part of the world are also drying up. Over-accumulation in the developed nations is, in large part, responsible for the lack of accumulation in the underdeveloped. Because profits can no longer sufficiently be increased by a further growth of capital in the industrially-advanced countries, they are also diminishing in the backward nations because of their lack of capital. To keep on exploiting the backward areas will slowly destroy their exploitability. But not to exploit them means to reduce even more the already insufficient profitability of capital in the advanced nations. They will thus try to increase rather than to relax their exploitation, if no longer in collaboration with the backward nation's traditional ruling classes, then by way of neo-colonialism, i.e., in collaboration with the new ruling classes that have been tossed up by the anti-colonial movements.

However, the continued indirect economic domination of the less-developed nations by Western capital offers no solution for the actual needs of the vast mass of their populations, nor will it solve the basic problem of profit-production for Western capitalism. All that it does is to sustain somewhat longer the viability of the disintegrating capitalist world economy, aided by the brutal suppression of all resistance caused by the unrelieved and growing social misery. It is quite safe to predict that at least in the underdeveloped part of the world the prevailing misery will lead to always new rebellions against the dominating foreign powers as well as against their native collaborators.

It is of course true, as Marcuse says, that the rebellions in the underdeveloped nations are not proletarian movements in the Marxian sense. Even if these national-revolutionary movements should succeed it would merely lead to social conditions such as characterize the capitalist world either in the East or in the West, where proletarian revolutions in the Marxian sense seems no longer a possibility. According to Marcuse, "the reality of the labouring classes in advanced industrial society makes the Marxian 'proletariat' a mythological concept; [and] the reality of present-day socialism makes the Marxian idea a dream."[55] There exists, however, no "present-day socialism," which, by its performance, proves the unreality of the Marxian concept of socialism, i.e., the class-less society free of economic value relations. Neither does the reality of the labouring classes in advanced industrial society deny the reality of the Marxian concept of the proletariat merely because their living standards have improved, and merely because their class consciousness has evaporated. As before, society is divided into owners of the means of production and the property-less working class, or in controllers of capital and the power-less wage-labourers.

It is only on the assumption that the *status quo*

can be maintained, that all social problems can be resolved within the existing institutions, that history has come to a stop in the established conditions, that it is possible to deny the proletariat—that is, the vast majority of the population in the industrially-advanced countries—a rôle in history, which can necessarily only be an oppositional rôle and thus must find expression in a revived, or newly-emerging, class consciousness. Of course, Marcuse does not deny further historical development; the factor of auto-mation alone, he points out, "signals the possibility of a revolution in capitalism." In his view, however, "this is a long process," so that "the revolution cannot be scheduled for today and tomorrow." It is for these reasons, that Marcuse provides his dismal prognosti-cations always with the rider—"in the foreseeable future." But what else is the "foreseeable future" if not the recognition of some basic trends which affect and alter existing conditions in a definite direction. The emphasis must then be put not on the possibly drawn-out persistency of existing conditions, but on the elements within these conditions which indicate their dissolution.

Marcuse seems to believe, and at the same to regret, that the recent and current conditions of working class "affluency" in the industrially-advanced nations are here to stay. The traditional Marxist explanation of the bourgeoisification of the labour movement as being restricted to a small labour aristocracy no longer holds true in Marcuse's view, because "changes in the system of work and rising standards of living have transformed the majority of the organized working class into a labour aristocracy, whereas in Lenin's day this was still no more than a small minority."[56] There has been, Marcuse says, a "split within the working class itself, turning nearly all the organized working class into a labour aristocracy,"[57] which has brought forth a "new kind of working class solidarity—solidarity between organized workers who have a job and a measure of security, as opposed to those who have no job and no chance of getting one in the foreseeable future either."[58]

This is not a new working class solidarity but the absence of all solidarity, for even within the organized sector of the working class—itself a minority—there is no solidarity but merely, though not always, a mutual agreement to respect the job monopolies of different unions. Labour unions simply have become reactionary because the market relations on which they are based are no longer progressive but regressive social relations. This is not a question of "social integration," where the interests of labour and capital coincide, but merely an example of the persistency of obsolete institutions in the decaying market economy.

But this persistency will not assure their present social position in times to come. As capital cannot gain anything from the unemployed, but must sustain them in one fashion or another, it can only gain, if gain it must, from the employed workers. It is very difficult, if not impossible, to undo once-reached living standards without calling forth serious social convulsions. Except in times of war, with government assuring social peace by military means, it has never really been tried. In the past, in times of depression, the pressure of the unemployed on the labour market largely sufficed to bring wages down to some extent. But effective unionization soon allowed a large segment of the working class to maintain their once-reached wage-scales. Instead of cutting their wages, their productivity was brought to a higher pitch, thus increasing the profitability of capital in spite of the so-called "stickiness" of wages. Under present conditions, and in the face of increasing automation, this means the progressive displacement of labour by capital.

The high standards of living reached in the industrially-advanced nations must themselves turn into detriments of capital expansion. For to maintain them under conditions of decreasing profitability implies the continuous extension of non-profitable production and this, in turn, an increasingly greater need to raise the productivity of labour, which, under present conditions, means the steady growth of unemployment. Unemployment itself becomes an increasing expense, which, in connection with all the other expenses of "affluency," will sooner or later tax to the utmost even the greatest "economic and technical capacities." The "affluency" will not be maintainable unless the nature of society itself is changed, unless the profitability principle is discarded. The very "affluency" and the social difficulties in the way of its reversal, will itself turn into a revolutionizing force.

This is not to say that "affluency" breeds revolution. It is only to say that no absolute impoverishment is required to produce oppositional sentiments. People need not be reduced to starvation levels before they begin to rebel; they may do so at the first deep inroads into their customary living standards, or when access to what they consider their living standards should be is denied them. The better off people are, the harder they feel any deprivation and the more tenaciously they cling to their accustomed style of life. It is in this sense that a partial loss of the prevailing "affluency" may be enough to destroy the existing consensus.

Marx says somewhere that "the proletariat is revolutionary, or it is nothing." Presently it is nothing and it may well be that it will continue to be nothing. But there is no certainty. Marx also said that "the ruling ideas are the ideas of the ruling classes," which does not prevent the rise of subversive ideas. Obviously, subversive ideas will flourish only under conditions of dissatisfaction. There is not enough dissatisfaction in present-day prosperous society, even if it is a false prosperity. Consequently, there is one-dimensional thought, a society without opposition. As nothing else can be expected under such conditions, we have not gone into Marcuse's penetrating critical analysis of the advanced industrial society's ruling ideology. Here we agree with all his observations and are thankful for them. Since Marx, it was to be expected, as Marcuse relates, that the "advancing one-dimensional society alters the relations between the rational and the irrational. Contrasted with the fantastic and insane aspects of its rationality, the realm of the irrational becomes the home of the really rational,"[59]—which is the final outcome of the fetishism of commodities and of capital.

Actually, however, and here Marcuse is himself a witness, non-fetishistic rationality still exists but can, for all practical purposes, be ignored. What opposition exists remains largely inarticulate. It cannot become a social force because it represents as yet no material interests strong enough to oppose the material interests represented by the ruling ideology— or ruling insanity. Where opposition ceases to have material force it ceases to be effective opposition. It becomes a luxury—the deeper insight of intelligent men who may well despise both society and its victims for defending so obstinately the prevailing irrationality. Yet, the impoverished minority must live within this irrationality and must accept it by necessity, which is then turned into an apparent virtue to make it more palatable. Even where opposition finds political forms it finds false expressions as, for instance, in the American Negro struggle for civil rights; a meaningless and, even in its meaninglessness, an unrealizable goal. The "outsider" cannot step outside existing conditions—unless he risks all, his very life, by arson and looting. But then he is already back on the road to a reality which is rational.

The sporadic rebellions of despair by small minorities are easily handled by the authorities representing the smug majority, which includes the mass of the proletariat. Black or white, "the substratum of outcasts and outsiders" can be decimated piecemeal by the very conditions of existence provided for them. But as their number grows—and it is growing—the frequency of their rebellious acts will also increase, as will the awareness on the part of many of the smug that perhaps they, too, will soon find themselves on the human refuse heap of capitalism. To judge by the past, the growth of social misery gives power to this misery and power leads to conscious actions to overcome misery. When Marcuse says with respect to the unemployables that "the economic and technical capabilities of the established societies are sufficiently vast to allow for adjustments and concessions to the underdog, and their armed forces sufficiently trained and equipped to take care of emergency situations,"[60] he correctly

describes the existing conditions in the industrially-
advanced countries. But what is true today is not
necessarily true tomorrow and will, in any case, be
less so if the trend of capitalist development proceeds
as it has in the past.

Of course, one cannot go by past occurrences. The
events of the past may not be repeatable; the age
of revolutions may well be over and the one-dimensional, stationary, totalitarian society unavoidable.
But if we cannot judge by past experiences we cannot judge at all. In that case, everything is possible—
even a proletarian revolution. This presupposes the
continued existence of the proletariat, which, however, is allegedly already in dissolution, not only
with respect to its disappearing class-consciousness,
but in its social functions as well. A distinction is
frequently being made between the "classical working
class," i.e., the industrial proletariat in the Marxian
sense, and the modern working population, of which
only the smaller part has productive occupations.
But this distinction is artificial, for what differentiates
the proletariat from the bourgeoisie are not particular
occupations among the former, but their lack of
control over their own existence through the lack of
control over the means of production. Whatever their
occupations, wage-workers are proletarians. Even if
more workers are now engaged in non-productive,
so-called service industries, their social position vis-a-
vis the capitalists remains unaltered. Due to the

concentration of capital and the elimination of the proprietary middle-class there are now more proletarians than ever before. It is of course true, that a good portion of these dependents receive incomes which provide them with either bourgeois or petty-bourgeois living standards. But the vast majority, as far as living standards are concerned, fall in the category of wage-workers, no matter how unproductive their work may be.

The working population may not think, or may not like to think, of itself as being proletarian and may, by this reluctance to recognize its social position, contribute to the one-dimensionality of the ruling ideology. However, in order not to lose their utility, all ideologies must in some way relate to factual conditions; if they lose all contact with reality they are on the verge of breaking down. While the well-paid employed worker may not recognize his proletarian status, the unemployed will do so more readily, and the impoverished, treated as an outcast, has no longer any choice. But to recognize one's class position does not mean to become class conscious in a revolutionary sense. It is merely a first condition for the development of an anti-capitalist ideology and movement.

When Marx spoke of the "historical mission" of the working class to end the capitalist system, he spoke, as may be gathered from his theory of accumulation, of the expropriation of the few by the many.

He rightly saw that the expansion of capital is also the polarization of society into a small minority of capitalists and a vast majority of property-less people forced to sell their labour power in order to exist, and unable to exist when it is no longer bought. The industrial proletariat of a hundred years ago has meanwhile swollen to an amorphous mass of wage-receiving occupations and professions, all of which are dependent on the vicissitudes of market events and the fortunes or misfortunes of the accumulation process. They may think of themselves however they like, but they belong not to the ruling but to the ruled class.

Capitalism is basically a two-class society, notwithstanding the various status differentiations within each separate class. The ruling class is the decision-making class; the other class, regardless of its inner differentiations, is at the mercy of these decisions, which determine the general conditions of society, even though they are formed with a view to the special needs of capital. The ruling class cannot act otherwise than it does; that is, stupidly or intelligently, it will do everything to perpetuate itself as a ruling class. Those outside the decision-making process may disagree with the decisions made, as they may not correspond with their own interests, or because of convictions that things should be done differently. But to affect or change these decisions they must have power of their own.

Whatever the decision-makers decide upon has to be actualized in the sphere of production, as the manner of distribution depends on that of production, and the patterns of consumption on the patterns of production. Without control over the productive process no decisions can be made, no class can rule. The control of production is exercised through the control of the means of production, by ideology and force. But neither property, nor ideology, nor force can produce anything. It is productive labour on which the whole social edifice rests. The productive labourers have more latent power at their disposal than any other social group, or than all other social groups combined. To turn the latent into actual power demands no more than a recognition of social realities, and the application of this knowledge in the pursuit of the producers' own ends.

To deny this fact is the main job of bourgeois ideology. It comes to the fore in its economic theories and in the general disparagement of productive labour in its tangible results. However, despite the prevalent notion of the decreasing importance of the industrial proletariat, more attention is devoted to it than ever before, because, actually, its potential power to control society was never so great as it is now. The technical-organizational "socialization" of production, i.e., that interdependency of the national production process and the absolute dependency of the whole of the population on an uninterrupted

D

flow of production, provides the working class with almost absolute power over the life and death of society. They could destroy society by simply ceasing to work. While this could not be their intention, being members of the same society, they could nevertheless shake society to its foundations if they were determined to alter its structure. It is for this reason that unions have been adapted to the capitalist establishment to control industrial disputes, that governments, including labour governments, pass anti-strike legislation, and that those most aware of the latent power of industrial action, that is, the totalitarian regimes, outlaw strikes altogether.

Because the industrial proletariat has the power to change society if so inclined, it is now, as before, the class on which the actual transformation of society depends. At this point, we are only pointing to this power, aside from the question as to whether or not it will or can, ever be used. For if this power did not exist, if its application was not a real possibility, there would indeed be no hope of overcoming the material forces of coercion by another material force. The only hope left would be the expectation that mere ideas could change both the ruling ideology and the material interest at its base.

However, all social struggles are also ideological struggles; yet, if they are to succeed, there must be a material lever to overturn the defences of existing society. It is not entirely inconceivable that the growing irrationality will lead to a widespread revulsion among the population at large, regardless of their class affiliations, and to a growing conviction that there is no longer any need for, nor any sense in, exploitative class relations, but that society could be so re-organized as to benefit all people and grant all of them a human existence. This would amount to a triumph of reason over irrational class interests, and to the self-liquidation of the ruling class. Short of such a miracle, a new society will have to be fought for with all available weapons both in the ideological sphere and in the field of real power relations.

There can be no doubt that in any social crisis large layers of the population, not usually counted with the working class, will nonetheless side with the latter in opposition to the ruling class. Even now, when the workers are still quite apathetic, students, intellectuals, and other members of the non-pro-prietary new middle-class display considerable political interest on apparently isolated issues, such as war, disarmament, civil rights, and so forth. But their protests remain ineffective until they can be combined with real political power, which can be provided only by the working population. If there can be no working class revolution, there can be no revolution at all.

According to Marcuse a working-class revolution can no longer be expected in industrially-advanced society. And even if it could be expected, control over the productive powers by "control from below" would, in his opinion, not lead to a qualitative social change. The notion of such a qualitative change, he says, "was valid, and still is valid, where the labourers were, and still are, the living denial and indictment of the established society. However, where these classes have become a prop of the established way of life, there ascent to control would prolong this way in a different setting."[61] In other words, the bourgeoisie and the proletariat are now interchangeable; no matter which class may rule nothing basically would be altered in the established way of life.

If the working class has become a "prop" of the established way of life, so certainly have all other other classes, and while the labourers' "affluency," which turned them into a "prop," may be considerable, it is nothing in comparison with the "affluency" enjoyed by other classes. There is still inequality in "affluency" and, consequently, a struggle over relative shares of the general "abundance." Within this competition nobody can be satiated and, in fact, all people feel themselves not "affluent" enough. Actually, of course, working class "affluency," even in the most industrially-advanced society, is still a rather shabby affair, to be achieved by some quite extraordinary exertions in the production process. Still, it seems enough to keep the workers satisfied, at least in the sense that they do not contemplate the advisability of social change. The hypothetical "control from below", which would leave things the way they are, will thus not be put to a test.

The whole idea stands or falls with the assumed ability of capitalism to maintain present standards of living for the working population. By all that has been said before, we denied capitalism this ability. To be sure, the actual situation still proves otherwise, but the actual situation proves no more than it itself. The question is where will we go from here; for despite the "affluency" in a small part of the world, the human condition in general becomes increasingly more obnoxious and intolerable. Nor can this be altered within the confines of capitalism, and the end of capitalism is conceivable only as the ending of social class relations, as the abolition of the proletarian class. The one-dimensional society is such only ideologically; in every other respect it is still the capitalism of old. Ideological conformity depends on conditions of prosperity; it has no staying-power of its own. But unless all theoretical reasoning should be entirely valueless, in so far as it allows for predictability it points to the demise not only of capitalistic prosperity but also to the end of capitalism itself.

The end of capitalism, while conceivable only as the simultaneous abolition of the proletariat, may be preceded by a mere state-capitalist modification of the capitalist system. Such a revolution would not be a socialist revolution, as it would only transfer the control of the means of production, and therewith of production and distribution, from the hands of property-owners to those of politicians organized as the state. The proletariat would remain a controlled class unable to determine its own destiny. This type of revolution has some credibility because it would appear as the logical end-point of the increasing government-determination of the economy and of social life generally, and because it follows the familiar pattern of previously-established state-capitalist systems, which are now quite generally perceived as socialist regimes. But in these latter systems the state-capitalist form came into being not in order to abolish the proletarian class but to aid in its quick formation. Socialist ideology is here employed to cover-up the intensified exploitation of labour, and it has some degree of plausibility because of the accomplished nationalization of the means of production. In industrially-advanced nations, however, state-capitalism would be as irrational a system as that which preceded it. The difficulties in these nations cannot be resolved by an increase in exploitation but only by ending the system of exploitation itself.

In these nations it is increasing productivity which destroys the profitability of capital and therewith the motive power for further capital development. This is so because capital appears here as private property under the sway of competitive market relations, wherein the drive for capital expansion controls the capitalists instead of being controlled by them. However, profits are surplus-labour and even if the profit-determination of capital formation comes to an end, the production process still requires labour and surplus-labour. With the state monopoly over the means of production, the relationship between labour and surplus-labour can be determined by government. It could regulate the production and distribution process with or without equity. Just as the authorities in capital-poor nations continue class relations in their state-capitalist systems, so the authorities of industrially-advanced countries could do likewise. They would not have the same "excuse," but they could create a political apparatus of repression which could do without an "excuse." Class relations could be maintained just in order to have a privileged class, and the planned economy could be a planned class society.

There would have been a revolution but not a socialist revolution. The mark of the latter is precisely the socialization of the means of production and therewith the producers' control of their product and its distribution. Without this, they merely exchange one form of wage-slavery for another, quite aside from the possibility that the one may be preferable to the other. Socialism can be realized only through the self-determination of the working-class, which incorporates all productive functions on which social life depends and by which it is enriched. The interests of society as a whole must determine the conscious organization of the social production process and the rational distribution of its products. To make this a possibility, there must be the disappearance of social control by a special class of controllers, and this requires new forms of social and production organizations, the efficiency of which will have to be evolved by trial and error. To speak of social change which would end the capitalistic way of life means to speak of a working-class revolution, for it is only this particular class, which, from the point of view of production, is able to transform society into a class-less and rational community.

No mere change of government could realize socialism. It requires a radical transformation of society with the producers themselves turned into decision makers. Its planning mechanism will have to be set up in such a way that planners and producers represent identical interests and will, in fact, be branches of one and the same production organization. Under conditions of abundance, such as characterize the industrially-advanced society, distribution could be free of all value considerations and in that sense "equality" could be realized. However, this is not the place to plead the feasibility of socialism, or to elaborate upon the new institutions it will require. All we are intent on saying at this point is that for socialism to succeed capitalism it will have to be the work of the producing class.

To come back to earth. With the record of working-class behaviour before us, the workers' indispensability for the actualization of socialism makes socialism even less accessible and apparently no more than a "Marxian dream." Yet, one has only to think of what in all probability is bound to happen without a socialist revolution in order to think of the possibility of a different kind of behaviour on the part of the labouring classes. What is bound to happen is in some measure already happening, and the quantitative projection of the present into the foreseeable future points to the utter utopianism of solving social problems by capitalistic means. The phrase "socialism or barbarism" states the only real alternatives; yet, a state of barbarism can again be altered by counter-forces rising up within it.

If class-consciousness depends on misery, there can be little doubt that the misery awaiting the world's population will go beyond anything thus far experienced, and that it will come to engulf even the privileged minorities in the industrially-advanced nations, who still think of themselves as immune to the consequences of their own activities. Because there are no "economic solutions" for the contradictions of capital production, "economic solutions" are being attempted by political means, but such as fit the socio-economic structure of capitalism. This

means that the destructive aspects of capital production take on an increasingly more violent character; internally, by more and more waste-production;
externally, by laying waste territories occupied by
people unwilling to submit to the profit requirements
of foreign powers which would spell their own doom.
While the general misery will increase, the special
situations of "affluency" will also dissolve, as the
blessings of increasing productivity are dissipated in
a slaughterous competition for the diminishing
profits of world production.

It is, of course, conceivable that nothing will move
the working population, that they would rather
accept whatever misery comes their way than rise in
opposition to the system responsible for it. However,
the absence of a revolutionary consciousness is not the
absence of intelligence. It is far more likely that the
modern working class will not indefinitely endure all
that the capitalist system has in store for it; there
may be a breaking-point where intelligence may
come to include class-consciousness. The readiness
to take revolutionary steps does not necessitate a
consistent oppositional behaviour prior to the first
independent act; an apathetic working class under
certain conditions can become an aroused working
class under different conditions. Because it is this
class which will most deeply be affected by a reversal
of the fortunes of capital production, or by capitalist
excursions into war, it may in all likelihood be the

first to break with the one-dimensional ideology of capitalistic rule.

But again, there is no certainty. There is only a chance—as Marcuse remarks in a somewhat different context. But it is only a chance not because part of the proletariat is left out of the capitalist integration process, but because capital may destroy the world before an opportunity arises to stay its hands. Integration in death is the only integration really given to capitalism. Short of this final integration, one-dimensional man will not last for long. He will disappear at the first breakdown of the capitalist economy—in the bloodbaths the capitalist order is now preparing for him. Capitalism, at the height of its powers is also at its most vulnerable; it has nowhere to go but to its death. However small the chances are for revolt, this is not the time to throw in the towel.

NOTES

1. H. Marcuse, *Socialism in the developed Countries, International Socialist Journal,* Rome, April, 1965, pp. 150-151.
2. *Ibid.,* p. 150.
3. *Ibid.,* p. 140.
4. H. Marcuse, *One-Dimensional Man,* Beacon Press, Boston, 1964.
5. *Ibid.,* p. XIII.
6. *Ibid.,* p. XV.
7. *Ibid.*
8. *Ibid.*
9. *Ibid.,* p. XIII.
10. *Ibid.,* p. XV.
11. *Ibid.,* p. XVI.
12. *Ibid.,* p. XVI.
13. *Ibid.,* p. 227.
14. *Ibid.,* p. 251.
15. *Ibid.,* p. 257.
16. *Socialism in the developed Countries,* p. 140.
17. R. Hilferding, *Das Finanzkapital,* Wien, 1910.
18. *Socialism in the developed Countries,* p. 139.
19. *Ibid.*
20. *Ibid.,* p. 141.
21. *Ibid.,* p. 144.
22. *One-Dimensional Man,* p. 154.
23. *Ibid.,* p. 144.
24. *Socialism in the developed Countries,* p. 140.
25. *Ibid.,* p. 148.
26. *Ibid.*
27. *Ibid.,* p. 149.
28. *Ibid.,* p. 150.
29. *Ibid.,* p. 149.
30. H. Marcuse, *Industrialization and Capitalism,* Brandeis University, 1965, p. 27.

31. *Socialism in the developed Countries,* p. 141.
32. *Ibid.,* p. 143.
33. *One-Dimensional Man,* p. 53.
34. H. Marcuse, *Soviet Marxism,* New York, 1961, p. XI.
35. *One-Dimensional Man,* p. 29.
36. *Ibid.,* p. 28.
37. K. Marx, *Grundrisse der Kritik der Politischen Öekonomie.* Berlin, 1953, p. 593.
38. *Ibid.,* p. 594.
39. *Ibid.,* p. 595.
40. *One-Dimensional Man,* p. 36.
41. *Ibid.,* p. 45.
42. *Ibid.,* p. 55.
43. *Soviet Marxism,* p. 67.
44. *Socialism in the developed Countries,* p. 142.
45. *One-Dimensional Man,* p. XI.
46. *Ibid.,* p. 144.
47. *Socialism in the developed Countries,* p. 149.
48. *Soviet Marxism,* p. 66.
49. *One-Dimensional Man,* p. 43.
50. *Ibid.*
51. *Soviet Marxism,* p. 174.
52. *One-Dimensional Man,* p. 42.
53. *Socialism in the developed Countries,* p. 146.
54. *Ibid.*
55. *One-Dimensional Man,* p. 189.
56. *Socialism in the developed Countries,* p. 145.
57. *Ibid.*
58. *Ibid.*
59. *One-Dimensional Man,* p. 247.
60. *Ibid.,* p. 257.
61. *Ibid.,* p. 252.